# COUNTRYSIDE
# CANADA

### BY
### James Wreford

*To Jessie*
*chauffeuse in all ten*
*provinces*
*and*
*companion*
*in every countryside*

Watson, James Wreford, 1915-
    Countryside Canada

(Fiddlehead poetry books; 280)

Poems.
ISBN 0-920110-67-3 pa.

I. Title.    II. Series.

PS8545.A845C69          C811'.5'4          C79-094604-1
PR9199.3.W375C69

# Contents

Introduction ................................................. 6
Peggy's Cove: NS ............................................ 7-9
Halifax....................................................... 10
Rock Barrens, Burin: Nfld. ................................. 11-14
Tantramar marsh: NB ....................................... 15-18
The Heron trail: PEI ........................................ 19-22
Cap Chat: PQ ................................................ 23
Pointe a la Croix, Gaspe: PQ ............................... 24-25
St Simeon Ferry: PQ......................................... 26
Fall Trees, the Gatineaus: PQ ............................... 27-28
Place Ville Marie, Montreal.................................. 29
Seasons at the Opinicon: Ont (Spring-Winter) .............. 30-33
Rideau farm, Chaffey's Locks: Ont .......................... 34
Watson's feed mill, Manotick: Ont .......................... 35
The bear on the Bancroft road: Ont ......................... 36
Bare woods, Bancroft ....................................... 37
Island Lake, near Thunder Bay: Ont ......................... 38-39
The CN Tower, Toronto....................................... 40
The Red River at St. Norbert: Man .......................... 41-42
Prairie skies on the Selkirk Trail: Man ..................... 43-45
Pioneer cemetery near Miniota: Man ........................ 46-48
Portage at Main, Winnipeg .................................. 49
Cathedral Grove: BC ........................................ 50-52
Pacific Rim Park, Ucluelet: BC .............................. 53-55
English Bay, Vancouver ..................................... 56
The Northlands, Peace River: Alta .......................... 57-59
The Northlands, Chemong: Sask ............................. 60-63
The Northlands, Ft. Prince of Wales......................... 64-70
The Northlands, Yellowknife: NWT ........................... 71
The Northlands, Old crow: YT ............................... 72
One people, one country .................................... 73-78

## Introduction

Sailing through fog
        or flying over ice-floes
is to come on a shore so stark
not to say grim, the heart
is all at one chilled, but
arrive when trees are a flame
of incredible beauty, and
heart's lifted high : this is
the challenge —
beyond the great grey glaciated rock
(endure enough)
and there's this wonder,
O all the air
singed with live hope!

### Peggy's Cove : NS
### (1)


People make places.
            What gives this place
its unique flavour
is the savour of courage and live sense:
I mean!
            to put up houses here in the rough
of the world and time
            on windswept rock
against the whip of salt spindrift
and
fog at the door's throat and in the window's eye
is defiance enough,
but to stand
steeple high about it
            —well—
            is nothing short
of consummate bravado, except that
spire, bell, church and people are
wily sea mongers at
getting the silver out
of even the wildest tides
            see
            the nets gleam
with the sheer sheen of
what drew men to this fishy dream.

## Peggy's Cove : NS
### (2)


Clinging to cliffs
the quays jut out, jostled by waves;
      man's held
between two arrogancies — rock and sea
but
himself unquelled
makes rock his gates and the sea his mews.
The crew-cut house
      above
    the dolled-up boat
     below
with coiled nets and with brilliant buoys
(marked by phosphorescent pennants)
       show
the contempt at once
of staid
    stone-based
      security
yet too
of the wild and unpredictable
inebriation of the sea.
Saying his Presbyterian prayers
     —but with
his prehistoric barbs —
     the fisherman
sails down the knife-edge between two fates
as only he, careless can
taking in himself
rock-firm assurance enough to be,
whatever should run against him,
      still
master of the Protean sea.

## Peggy's Cove : N.S.
### (3)


The flame-seethed, quick and simmering sea
that yet can be a darkness and a dread
moves as a woman's breast is moved
                         with swift
delight
            chased by despair:
                  here are cried
tenderness, pain, anger, love
                  —all
that makes the rock-rooted and storm-threshed
        beauty of
these stark homes real,
each heart shaken by fear but meshed
into the always returning hope.
This clutch of clapboard on a spine of stone
takes the full fury
        (but out of that all the aliveness)
                      of
those deep waters drawn
by guile and ingenuity
to the nets of faith.
                To live here is
to pluck from the strength of rock
enough
to take on the strength of seas.

## Halifax : N.S.

Rock, tide, time and root,
(given this shaping hand)
stand in new strength
                —the *citadel*
of the aspiring mind;
run      with the sudden quicksilver
of a new dream
                —the *quayside* of
far worlds drawn near;
                exhibit
the new proof
divergencies can
in high *assembly* meet;
                grow in
the *commons* of new joy where children make
all races one.

Cry on the wind this beauty called
from earth and air
by the first faith of men
                who saw
what could rise here.

### Rock barrens, Burin : Nfd.
### (1)


Bare, pared to the bone
grey, grim
robbed of its former green
           this jut of rock
rises like some great dead rolled-over whale
out of the sea's wrack.
Whipped by wind
snakes of dust rise, fall;
lashed by rain
soil is runnelled and washed out
and will not come again.
The sawdust tells the tale,
           mounds of it,
              at the hill foot
rotting, year on year,
the mortal remains of what
was once the green sweet life
that in the rock found root.
Clear-cut by man
            the ruin
sans bush, sans bird
             stands mute
a waste of air and light
world of misrule.

Deserts there are but none worse than
the desert of the soul.

### Rock barrens, Burin : Nfd.
### (2)

After cloud's torn
the sun rays out over the wet waste
until stone seems
a shine of colours not seen before —
the flash of mica gleams
from the glint of schist,
                    the fire
of quartz veins the rough gneiss,
even pitted limestone glows,
the granite has a thousand eyes;
but above all
                    mosses spring up
vivid as red-tipped flame
                    and the grey
lichens flick out, lipped with gold.
One knows the day will come again
when this sweet press
spreading across the waste space
will catch the seeds of a still more live
future of green grace.

### Rock barrens, Burin : Nfd.
### (3)


Lacking the heroic myth
that
    out of some golden age
can get from the past
      power enough
to face the rage
     despair
        doubt
           guile etc.
of desperate time
we none the less have
Canada,
    this strength to climb
from the land-slip and split scree
of torn time
      to the live hill
renewed with all the wonder of
the wood-green will.

**Rock barrens, Burin : Nfd.**
**(4)**


Trees have a way with rock
they split even the hardest hold
with tenderness,
      letting the root work
with the insinuation of a faith
won't rest
until it comes out at last
the green leaf and the power
of this delight —
      children that pluck
out of the cracked rock
      the budding flower.

### Tantramar marsh : NB
### (1)

See the marsh
          — flood full —
sun running alive on
the channeling tide
with the gulls gone
          wing wild
where waves work back
into the slack creeks
crying the joy
that the whole plain speaks
on the return of
the brimming grace
makes this
        O
            such
                a
such
      a
        green place:

let the heart so thirst
the hour can't hold
the tide out longer
              quick
suck the wild up
                fold
this marvel in
so that
        dry harsh stricken
though time may be
                we
shall have our own
         tide-green marsh.

### Tantramar marsh : NB
### (2)

This ache of emptiness
that here in the wide marsh
      moves the dyked heart,
calls for the thrust of the returning tide.
When will we be a part
of the quick in life again
      the streams
struggling to maintain themselves
      the sea
riding in
      august with brimming light
up every course —
      till we
feel in our bones the conturbation of
being free once more
      torn,
         yes,
choked,
      overwhelmed,
         but O
with what
      what loveliness!

### Tantramar marsh : NB
### (3)

To come out of the dark woods
on this sheet of light —

         the sea-shot marsh
on fire with gold
        the air alive
with the high
     harsh
       quarrel of gulls
at the turned tide —
is like the ached-for at last world
our constricted and confined ways
have yearned for,
our wings furled too long
that now
     like the wild hawks
can ride the free wind;
        ride, ride
the unrestricted joy, O heart, of
days opened wide.

### Tantramar marsh : NB
### (4)

Be the fierce hawk the freedom of
the wide marsh looses —
                             sight made keen
body a wind-slip construct
neat, fine, lean
made lovely, as it is,
                             by the need
to ride

              the
                    veering
                              wind
and strike
              unblinded by the light
into the blind dark
of the marsh's depth
                              and there
come on its prey
                              rid the hay of
what preys on it
                              and thus prove
a gleaner keeps the whole land clean
finding
              between terror and corruption
that beauty men stand to stare
                                   —look!
and stare again at.

### The Heron trail : P.E.I.
### (1)

Once this divided isle
simply raised trees, grazed deer
man came to it with
arrow and spear

flintlock, mortar, fort
war shook the air
Indian, French, British made
anger, guile, despair

and yet the base of the
first beauty remains —
hill, wood, above
the marsh-fringed plains,

and slowly over the flags
that mark man's boasted day
the indifferent heron takes
his great-winged, arrowy way.

### The Heron trail : P.E.I.
(2)


Red soil
          blue seas
                    green-alive fields
who would have thought that here
such ferocity
could strike from the air
nevertheless
the heron that
takes up his placid place
                    blue murder shoots
into the tidal race!
Yet,
        lacking all this,
                  how
could the perfection of his line
halt us
        — amazed at such grace
given among men?

### The Heron trail : P.E.I.
### (3)


Necessity
has the real beauty
the heron made for
spearing his prey
here the perfection of
shape
      form
            line
is of the essence;
no other design
than knife-like beak
a snake's head
fire in the eye
could nail dead
the silver agony
of the pierced fish.
This work for,
                 this
wonder unleash.

### The Heron trail : P.E.I.
### (4)


To wait an hour for this
sharp strike and silver flash
the heron on his stiff stilts
stands in the wash

of the ascending or
outgoing tide
imperturbable but
dagger eyed

part of the fierceness that
Canada, out of your nursed calm
can with the beauty of
terror flame.

## Cap Chat : P.Q.

Loom out of the mist
great cliff
          the abrupt end
of our long conspiracy against change
harbour us among
the fire-veined
          and hardened
               strata that
have worn out time
and still
headland on headland climb
from the weather of
endless shift and chance;
be the cliff-clear
          for us too
            O longed-for
permanence.

### Pointe à la Croix, Gaspé : P.Q.
### (1)


Far down the dark bay
                        the bright spire
draws the land to it
                        in
a sudden assurance that
wood
        field
                fence
                        road
                        will win
to the pure sky at last
(however thick
                weed-grown
                        fallen
                                stray)
because this faith once put
pain and sorrow high.

This is the country
where the cross is at the centre
                                see
where all paths meet
                        it soars
setting men free
from any anguish
less than eternity
                        here
time climbs
to a height beyond despair.

### Pointe à la Croix, Gaspé : PQ
### (2)

People
    bowed with care
        but with clear eyes
having 'made land' from thick stubborn spruce
put bells in the sky
        whose joy peals
over fields flagged with
        flower de luce.
Catholic and French
        but more than that
a race which has taken from the earth
the strength to suffer time
and found in the soil made over,
        their rebirth:
further,
wintered on hardness
they've sucked the sweet of summer
        such
as in their eyes
        —look!—
        shines through
whatever doubt or grief may cloud us,
to clear skies.
The great bell tolls,
        joy takes the field
from the once dark wood
        now opened up
foals run
        cattle low
        renewing man
has built his new-world hope.

### St. Simeon ferry : PQ


The strength is
       —no,
            not rock,
                  but *will*
but what broke the rock up
to make this tight-cribbed harbour
                out of which
man sails to take
the wealth of the fish-quick seas;
                but *faith*
that saw in this hard land
the base
out of the storming seas to net
a touch of grace;
                 but *hope*
that,
      as in the spire which draws
              sea
                 land
                    to climb
to the sky here, men may
make a new earth and time.

### Fall Trees, the Gatineaus: PQ
### (1)


Not fire compares :
     this flame
is like an old man's fierce
cry against time
      his last chance
to coerce
blood
   bone
     the deeps in him
to declare
he is the master yet
and wonder of the air
before he goes—
     his is
the year at the high peak!
Of this great burning
through this still fierce root—
(more than the on-fire forests make
against the hard shot of
wintering frost and sleet
snow ice barrenness)
who could cease to speak?

     This
cry
     this
assertion that
   beauty is all
(whatever else fails)
     this
won't, can't fail.

### Fall trees, the Gatineaus : PQ
### (2)


Why *so* gold
              *so* red?
The heart would have been stirred with less:
why has the world to be
the non-pareil of loveliness
and what is it in us
              cries
smitten to tears
                    with this awe
                        this amaze
that grips
              grips us
at mere trees turned red
                        turned gold?
We know
there's nothing here except
a fire touched off by frost.

Yet however inept
our reasoning may be
                    the soul
feels a high wonder here
              that is
in leaf and branch
                    and the singed air
a meaning and a voice.

### Place Ville Marie, Montreal : PQ

This is the flower of
    —this tower—
      hope
       faith
here in the city that
men warped from
     sea
      forest
       rock
making a world where
   we'll be —
     all we may be!
The nature of man is to tower
out of nature to a new time
    where
from earth
   water
     air
      he can
to his own sky climb
lit with his signs.
      See them
   flash!
power and delight, delight and power
day and night O night and day
   his
at last proved hour.

## Seasons at the Opinicon : Ont.
### Spring


To see the snow's edge break
crumble
      melt back
           retreat
               rot
day by quickening day
and watch the shining sheet
of alive water run
down gullied soil
         and hear
the whole land come to voice
before even birds appear
O cracks
      O cracks
         the heart!
How can the race stay hard
in disbelief
      worse, in despair
      when
the field's bared
to the rising sun,
        soon
the light will wink
    not on
snow coated with ice
      but
butterflies gone crazed
with their new joy
and we with
    —sudden—
      the swift delight
of summer-returning birds
can fly the night.

### Seasons at the Opinicon: Ont.
### Summer


The long day burns on the gleaming rock
the water quivers as though the lake
simmered with fire
dragon flies —
                    their quick wings flashing —
                                        make
the air a woven brightness;
fish leap in arcs of light;
                    above —
the high peace of noon doves
                    sounds in still woods,
swallows in turning
                    white the sky:
here all the live-long hour
in deep-feathered grass lie back
                    gaze
at the high pomp of
summer-green great-crowned trees
and hear the cricket sing
                    the clack
of hoppers on the wing
                    the hum
of bees in clover.
What could more ever sum
                    contentment up?
The noon
                    towers and belfries of
                            cloud built high
                    Ontario,
where
are richer hours?

**Seasons at the Opinicon: Ont.**
    **Fall**


The cry against time these trees make is
red in our hearts too:
                    make now
            the fierce
hour of seed and splendour
before the frosts arrive
                    that pierce
into the root and bone.
Let the end be
        this marvel!
What matter if leaves fall
            and the bare
pitiful gaunt days come on us of
                    pain and grief
we've had this moment:
the world has been
                rich beyond thought.
        So much so,
this wonder is all that counts
this gift of grace
                that will not go.

**Seasons at the Opinicon: Ont.**
**Winter**


First snow!
The tired land becomes
all its sweet childhood once again
such as we
    too
      knew
when faith was white
       and our hearts were clean.
Flake on flake fill the nostalgic air
with the returned innocence of a world
in which
     worn rock
     split tree
        the sagging roof
and rotting verandah
     are
furled, folded away, forgot
in the marvel of
   this new page
       presented us.
Write on it now
no longer the wandering steps of doubt
nor the too extravagant vain vow
but
the dream we dreamed of once
walking within the snow-soft woods
on paths of child-like wonder
    when
all our thought was gentleness
but *all* our thought
      was gentleness.

**Rideau farm, Chaffey's Locks: Ont.**


Nothing but sheer courage
could have matched this stony land
        here was
sternness for sternness,
               the firm intent,
the iron mind.
        This man has
the country in him
             of a wintered faith
ice has knocked at his heart,
the rock of his will
            will wear out rock:
yet his chief part
is to gentle the scene.
        About his house
flowers grow
        in cribs
            of soil-filled stone
primula
        and phlox
           and marigold
he tends them one by one.

## Watson's feed mill, Manotick: Ont
### (a museum)


Time
    and the tide of fortune
                may indeed
have robbed the old mill of
its intended first function
        but
it still stands here
            the proof
stones are the business that
imagination puts them to:
           now
they serve to mill out memories
green in continuing hope.
      Sing how
we plucked this power
  out of the ignorant stream
to bruise the grain
  raised from mere wilderness
fed lowing Frisia, Guernsey, Ayr
and all the far geographies
       Canada
of a countryside rich in
contributary sweet countrysides —
old mill clack on still
    graced in our minds
with all our remembered prides.

### The bear on the Bancroft road: Ont.


The brash pride with which these boys
bear
      straddled across the roof-rack of
their shooting-brake,
                        the shot
black bear
                   (proof
of their prowess with
                person-to-person radio
telescopic sights
and high-velocity rifles)
               O
shines
        shouts from
their laughing self-conceit, as
they streak down the north-country trail
Indians once took
(hunger having driven these
on the hunt of native need)
boasting between beers
— the cans thrown out—
the kill they made.
The bear hangs helpless
                its great head
rolling from side to side
             its tongue
lolling out of its foam-flecked mouth
its legs splayed
its eyes stung by flies—
         no longer king
of the forest glades:
             but split
eviscerated
        a trophy for
the sheer hell of it!

### Bare woods, Bancroft: Ont

Hunter, look behind:
>             fear is
upon your track;
*you* are the wolf now
>             the world is after.
O ravening man
>             against *you* is bent the bow.
The land you've ravaged so
>             will rise
indignant from its indignities,
you will become the stark waste
from which you've stripped the trees
the bared woods in you cry out
>             their weed-grown ways
life melt from you and yours
>             as from
polluted stream and lake
the root go dry in you as in
rock flayed by erosion where
no seeds take:
the barrens in the mind and heart
will spread until the land
at last is avenged —
>             and you,
in fear
>       in despair,
>             must stand.

## Island lake, near Thunder Bay: Ont.
### (1)


To dive into these waters or
rest in these woods isn't now enough:
carry them back, have them walk
beside you the reproof

of unclean ways, of times that are
arid and profitless and waste.
Let the clean lake reach up
into your city haste

the trees put out their branches in
the heat of your affairs,
and all your climate from today be
these bird-excited airs.

**Return from Island Lake: Ont.**
(2)


Return you must —
　　　　　　　but turn
with the wild still on you:
　　　　　　　　　　walk
the city streets as one having just
had talk with wonder
　　　　　　　　　whose eyes
still shine from sunlight on the lake
and the great clouds melting there,
　　　　　and noon
an ache of high cicadas crying
before the shadows come,
and bees spilled out on flowers.
Let their rich honey stay with you,
let hours
when all at once
the world and self were one
　　　　　　　　　and you
knew at the heart things could and did
ring true
step back with you
　　into the fret and fume
make here
an inner and secret wood
　　　　　　　　　far from
the all too troubled air —
then walk the streets at last
free for what must be done
deep in you having the
　　　　　seed
of an unvarying noon.

### The C.N. Tower, Toronto: Ont.

What tall mullein stalk
                in far green fields
lit by the flash of dragonflies
on long hot noons
                in the cicada-high
          cry
of sweet summer skies
flowers like this,
              O beauty of
creating man —
              this sheer-rise pride
of the towering and metalled mind
built from rock
              but rock magnified
crystallized
            given new grace:
rock -eyed with vision
              rock -crowned with light
rock -opening doors to dreams
              such as
lead out of night,
rock —
            raised above rising mullein stalks
to the poetry of the high
           and burning noon-heart
              where *man*
fills the whole sky.

### The Red River at St. Norbert: Man.
### (1)


The edge of calm
           where the slow waters coil
           is at the same time
(but knock, but mill)
           the
agitation of distress;
           you flow
subsuming all troubles,
           smoothing down
ripples that fish make
           leaping to
           the fly-filled air

yet
sucking in
unwary insect to striking predator.
Here is the dilemma —
           as peace builds up
loop by loop more beauty
           the more
it draws in those who prey on it:
           the sedge
flicker with dart-
        ing
           dragon-
       fly
kingfishers strike into the astonished stream
and
      swallows
           evening-
     murder
           burnished
     the
           sky.

### The Red River at St. Norbert: Man.
### (2)


The enriched plain is
layered with silt on silt
             of floods
that have made more green
the land they built.
Destruction lines each bank
your stream is red with war
and
though men push their levees up
more is to come,
                  and more.
Each overflowing loop you make,
             unmakes;
         here trees
are uprooted,
          soil slips,
                      house/byre
are swept to their bankcruptcies.
Yet out of this
             more seed
more grass, grain,
             *beauty,* grow:
buoyed with the destroyer and destroyed
your teeming waters flow.

## Prairie skies on the Selkirk Trail: Man.
### (1)


The wonder of this wideness
                          of this
illimitable reach of sky
unblocked by forest,
                          not shut out
by the mountain-tricked eye,
leads between blades of grass
in this low and
                  unfeatured place
to the surprising prides the prairies can
grace us with,
                    that trace
far-sheeted stratus
                      broken through by
cornucopias of
                  heaped cumulus
and
high over all
the pure fire of cirrus
lifting us to those blues
made still more intense
                          more burning still.
Gaze into these majesties
and what is all your doubt
                            your grief
your human pettiness?

## Prairie skies on the Selkirk Trail: Man.
### (2)


Prairies provoke dimensions:
                              here men
see far,
              think big,
                              stretched by
lines that run out of view
                  or
feel dwarfed,
                  encircled by the sky —
in either case they are made aware
of the sky in them
                              of dreaming space
                              or circumscription
                  i.e.
the limits of their own minded place.

Long for long-distance and the call
of the drawing-on road,
                              drawing out of us
lengths never known:
                              we could be
we
pace-makers for the race!

### Prairie skies on the Selkirk Trail: Man.
### (3)


This burning unalleviated blue
arching the hot unbounded plain
is the last enemy,
inviting the flawless reign
of without-end
            uniformity.
No wonder men have here
planned their autocracies of the general good—
the social utopias
            where
all is levelled to the same plane
ruled by unclouded truth!
                        But
thank God
    *St. Malo* differs about it
from *Gnadenfeld*
            while the
    *Vikings* put their own republic up
and in the meantime
    *McTavish* has had its hard-cash way:
never did sky look down on
men with such an individual say!

## Pioneer cemetry near Miniota: Man.
### (1)


The poor
       the long-without-hope
              the scourged
came here
not only the landless man for the manless land
       but the man less rights
            less justice
     for the land less plan
less prospects
     less the needed dream.
The rich black earth

             wasted on the Indian hunt
cried out for plough and seed;
          the unused floods,
for dam and channel
and waters spent on swallowing grain;
           unbounded space
for the traffic of our needs
not least in ideas repressed too long
free to rise here into the sky's pride.
Keep this place
still sacred to
     both the longed-for end
     and the at-hand grace.

**Pioneer cemetry near Miniota: Man.**
                (2)


In sod huts, shacks, tents
                        the despised
who did not despise the ardours of their task
first set up home here
to turn this black tousled tough soil
to all that man could ask,
their tears their tools
                their wrongs their driving power
with,
        at the far end of the furrow,
                                hope.
Never forget the hour
now that affluence roofs the too-respected head
when bitterness was in the root
injustice and inequality and dread.

Go tenting for fun,
                sure!
                        Hire an old shack
by the duck-loud lake,
pile your car with the shot geese
                (fat on fall stubble fields)
pour out the rye with that spit-roasted deer,
it's great to get back to the simple life,
                                true!
But O recall the first simplicities
of hunger
                need
                        faith
                                labour
                                        *will*
that gave us all this ease.

### Pioneer cemetry near Miniota: Man.
### (3)


Cry the new man
ploughed in, sown, thrusting up
      no matter what
frosts winds storms angers
                despairs
hold the race
in stultified and repressed hope
        we
have toiled wept suffered enough
been kept back tricked trodden brutalized
in enough anguish
not to lean and bear down on time
with this fierceness to win through;
      no wrong now
no guile
      no injustice in high places
          no mis-applied power
can stop us
      who
have the green heart to suck up from our woe
harvests of thick grace.
Don't fear
      this will yet appear
          the sweet elected place.

## Portage at Main, Winnipeg: Man.


Towers high above
this point of maximum access
                    the
forever reaching hope
makes a new sky,
watch men lift
suddenly their eyes up
the image is of
ascending power:
given such centredness
                    even
the vacant plain can find
                    meaning
                    know
the focussed mind.
What rises here links
the rich but land-locked seed
with the far running tide
of the world's need.
Its streets go straight
to the heart of the matter —
                    this
faith that gives
            mere dust
                    vain skies
a meeting place and goal
                    :—
the once-bound plain is
stretched to take in
Russia, China, India
                    the
whole of man.

## Cathedral Grove: B.C.
### (1)


The amazing mechanism of
these giant redeemers of the world
taking from
the so polluted
           not to say
                poisoned air
spewed from our sins
the bloom of blue-tipped fir
          and the fired larch
will in the end save us
and in us too
          prevail.
We too must
buy back the used-up land
be the fir's renaissance
            tower
the larch of remedial beauty
            take
the tired hour
           the exhausted day
and from the spent air make
the gorgeous green again —
no longer drawing in
the sweet of life to give
weariness and waste,
          but win
like bud and leaf
           out of the worn world
      wonder
turning the done times
into this grove of green deliverance
towers in our limbs.

## Cathedral Grove: B.C.
### (2)


The essence is
this green
without this magic touch
rock would not flower
          nor
sun seed overmuch.
Mists creep through the firs
          caped and fringed with moss
in river-cuts the hard rock shows
this is a stern-visaged place
but
stronger than the tides
                  of Pacific storm
flows this sweep of cedar
              and spray
of tossed spruce.
The ability to extract from air
leaf
        moth
          bird
the calm
        of the last word
here is what we must
manufacture, enough
burning in us
                  lust
to bring the hour of love
to the large laziness
of the assured day
when we can lie all the long noon
                all the noon long
lost to the world's say.

## Cathedral Grove: B.C.
### (3)


The needed power
is now to raise
from the waste and worn world
                    of our own undoing
the somehow
                sweet
                        reborn
green hope
will through us grow
and make time bloom again,
drawing from
root-pierced rock
and sucked-in renewing rain
the beauty
            O the beauty
to put against our grief.
The equation is
to make of ourselves
                    the leaf
will take in time's wasted
                    worn
breathed-out anguish
                and
create out of these
                    food for
a new land
be indeed
            each
the photosynthetic I
will catch up the done earth to
$C_6H_{12}O6 + 6O_2 =$
            $6CO_2 + 6H_2O + E$
(for energy)
a living sky.

## Pacific Rim Park, Ucluelet: B.C.
### (1)


Shaken by storm
                    the thrust-out cliffs
bruised broken
                    stand
yet stronger and more enduring for
their anguish:
                    this is a land
huge with affliction
                    yet strangely more
lovely for that
                    more full of grace—
as in this race
its symbols down
                    the eagles fallen
                    the totems in the grass
who still keep high the dignities
in their still-prided ways.
Look how the long low Pacific light
fingering the mountain face
picks from the strata of time's grief
a beauty that wears out time;
just so
                    men's anguished vicissitudes
may
          to a lit wonder
                              climb.

## Pacific Rim Park, Ucluelet: B.C.
### (2)

The gaunt all but stripped firs
the scream of birds over burst seas
the leap of arrowed fish in firths
shattered to screes

and over the shadowed land huge
thunderheads piling through the shot heat —
no wonder the savage world found cry
in totemic threat

where great-beaked eagles and snorting whales
thrust their contempt of time
into the teeth of storm, and man
could with them climb

into the eye if not of hope
then courage at least or, in the end
the grim will to contend and still
contend.

            Watch this race ride
the tides out (the shifts, the guiles
the anger, the destruction) with
their own unyielding wiles

their faces worn but still unwearied, lined
but deep down alive still
                   see, they still wear
the power to wring from time what will
keep time in despair.

### Pacific Rim Park, Ucluelet: B.C.
#### (3)


Immense
this great cedar stood
before the foundation of the state
its time-resisting strength
fed from the thick rains
                        brought
by shining tides
deep in between
                        the rocky shores
its firm root making holds
to keep the years at bay,
its coarse and shaggy bark
                        marked by bear claw
rubbed by stag horn
                        struck
by lightning
stripped for wear by Indians
cloaking themselves against
the sweep of repeated storm:
here
            Canada
you come up to your height
this is the form
rock
        tide
                    and time
                                    have made,
and root kept green.
Keep it so,
                rise straight
                        tower clean.

### English Bay, Vancouver : B.C.


The high-rise totems of the new elite
soar over English Bay
                              in block on block
the symbols of
                    eagle raven shark
that we still
                    in our own way
                                        hold proof
of the main virtues —
the keen eye
                    to our own advantage
the tearing beak
                    quick to live off misfortune
            and most
the ruthlessness can wreak
our will and way in the threshed seas
of human turbulence:
                    yet how they shine —
a beauty which alone
                        this fury
                                    this drive
could own.

### The Northlands, Peace River: Alta.
### (1)


The valley
a sheer
      *incandescence*
                  all at once
of fall aspen
        turned pure gold
           glows
with a furnaced beauty:
nothing but
the bitter north
could hold such a fierceness out
        of such a wonder
it's as if this hour
was meant to stop the mouth
of all time's grief

cry if we must
                not the fear
of the long winter waiting us
but this short marvel which
           has in it all
      all
    loveliness.

## The Northlands, Peace River: Alta.
### (2)


Mad with butterflies
                    the flower-starred field
of this high-north alfalfa land
makes of the fall of time
all at once
                time's stand!
What day's more
          —but I mean—
                      crazed
with the sheer happiness
              of being alive
than this storm of winged wonder
                  loosed
in the bloom-rich plain?
For this
         spring burst the iron-hard ground
            with its tender green,
the seethed-with-summer air
                for this
made sap run nectar;
         let
the wine of the year's joy
              in us, too
a wing-drunk prairie get.

## The Northlands, Peace River: Alta.
### (3)


Look how
in the long low northern light
evening calls out the land,

            houses wink eyes
            walls leap to view

      hills
are tricked in sheer silk:

            there is
a living glow along the valley's rim
even the gullies shine,

            wind in the hay
is like a play of colts,

            sleughs shimmer like
quick dragonflies,

            clouds go by
belly-side blown,

            trees too seem all underskirts
            swung in a golden breeze
men scissor their shadows in huge lit strides
women are haloed in flame in the last rays.

Pity the South with its shut-down eves,
here summer goes into the midnight hours
the low and slanting light

            fingers the land
            with lingering care.
Where else will you find the like
        where
are the fields so pearled
the valley side beaten from silver

                  so?
However doomed, by what return of winter,
        here
is an hour not matched in pride.

### The Northlands, Chemong: Sask.
### The Aspen belt
### (1)


Aspen stand slim delicate
*vivant,* girls of grace
chatting perpetually in
fritillaries

of this-way, that-way leaves,
their long lithe limbs
in an agitation of sun —
until the whole day brims

with their unaffected, indeed
unwitting, loveliness.
Passing them, here's
a beauty, O world, can't pass.

### The Northlands, Chemong: Sask.
### The Aspen belt
### (2)


The nubile beauty of
these slender trunks
half hid by
                shimmering leaves
can make
                aspen plead
a gentleness
                moves
as the innocence of girls
the hard-rock
                heart

Here is
a world that foils
in its affecting tremor
                and
bared simplicities
the sharp-edged
                brittle
                        bitter
anger
                of our days.

### The Northlands, Chemong: Sask.
### The Aspen belt
### (3)


In their contempt of time
the shim-
          mering
                aspen
                     make
a beauty of the hard bare ground
nothing
can shake
                not storm
                not the returning frost
                not blackening fire
                     or worse
                man's desecrating agency:
the aching seed will nurse
in cracks
                in crevices
                          in joints
split by ice,
                in outwash
                  spread
                        by tumbling spates,
                in lanes
                     licked by devouring flame,
                in the dead
landscape of his heaps and holes
left by destroying man,
the tremor of sweet hope
                and, at last,
                     the lasting green.

### The Northlands, Chemong: Sask.
### The Aspen belt
### (4)


Be then
this shaken out
       and
teasing of bright light
       in
the stirred
      never stilled
         aspen
spill their spun
      wonder of
         quick grace:
spring out of the stiff
      and O
      still
        too
stony a ground
to this quiver of hope
      will
catch every hat-full of wind
      with
winks of sheer
      shown
        joy
at being just so
      so!
        lovely grown.

### The Northlands, Ft. Prince of Wales
### The Barrens
### (1)

North of the last spruce
     snow
forms the geometry
gives the land shape,
       cold
is the architect now
we
get down to the bare bones
of line and shape
           here
the ultimate simplicities
    of apex, plane appear
not the
      isosceles
     feathered at
     the edges
      as in
       firs
serating the horizon with
            tossed green
but basic rock
      plucked
    stripped down
     to the core
clean-cut, sheeted by ice
     skeleton clear.

Give us this power — the bleak
and barren hour that can
strip us again down to
    the fundamental
      man.

### The Northlands, Ft. Prince of Wales
### The Barrens
### (2)


Moss turns brittle
                    stalks of grass
          sheeted with ice
make a dry clack
               and
rattle in the wind
               the dark's back
          no birds pass.
What is it in the end
after leaf flower are gone
bird song is done
and the snows descend
will leave us
          enduring form?
Give us this to keep
               even if
cold
     storm
               and the fierce hand of ice
are the last test.
From coast to coast
bitter extremities
search out each weakness, fault;
bleakness cuts at
          each node, joint
               that
(split, imperfect, spoilt)
summer had failed to seal
               Yet
out of all this can
                    (pared down enough)
step the man will be
     more true, more real.

### The Northlands, Ft. Prince of Wales
### The Barrens
### (3)


Here is the beauty of
ice-plucked rock, wind-bared root
the tested outline, the basic shape,
that will last out,

what is our true form
without distractions or
excrecencies, minus the
furbelows — just as we are

with nothing to say for us but
that which will endure
rock-fast beneath the ice
against storm, root-sure.

## The Northlands, Ft. Prince of Wales
## The Barrens
## (4)


Such a short sojourner here
   the green
is soon replaced
    snow
      steps in
   ice
takes back the soil into its grip
   the wind
     is razor keen
and cuts cruelly into everything
     not furred
the long night of the wolves
closes about
    worse still
   the heart
seeks out the midnight caves
we shut ourselves in our lodges
   the encamped mind
    takes over
yet this
is the hour of
   tested seed
  of what lasts,
 of the necessitous
   craving
to break through,
  of what is the
    O
   glory
  that can
  *will*
rise from dark storm bitterness despair
and come again
    sweet.

## The Northlands, Ft. Prince of Wales
## The Barrens
## (5)


Start from inside.
                    Find again
          the essence.
Let it out — this deep
innermost fire that won't
be smothered
          keep
the heart alive, even if
the long night's come.  We have
          no beauty now
to speak for us
the land is like a grave
gone the delicate leaf
   the feathered grace is gone
harried by wind
          drifted with snow
          our joy is done
yet the deserts of wintryness
that have turned the streams still,
can't silence
          can't hold back
forever the green will.


Let the deep springing stir
the first, last things in man
          rise yet
the wonder is
     (come frost, come dark)
                    we can
still know the amazing
                    green
                         valley of
singing streams
          here in the heart
and still find here
the summer of bee-quick dreams.

### The Northlands, Ft. Prince of Wales
### The Barrens
### (6)


As the day shortens
                  faith
lengthens, an inner light
irradiates hill, plain
stars crowd the night

as the cold deepens
                    grace
heightens in us, can pierce
with a new gentleness,
is green-blade fierce

as the land hardens
                    hope
quickens, the deep spring
shall (watch you!) a more
incorrigible beauty bring

        to the last
        loved
        land of
the still green heart
                    where
        believe me
sweet summer won't depart.

### The Northlands, Ft. Prince of Wales
### The Barrens
### (7)

Sheeted with flowers
                     the barrens now
put by the pall of their all too long
             non-life:
             hear how
around the sleugh the piping frogs
cry the first days of spring
             the melt
is making the stiff ground sing
under the snow
                   the runlets voice
the joy that the year is on the move
            ice rots in the marsh
             the midge come out
             the air
             is suddenly alive
the silences of the long snow break
in the wonder of birds again
            willows burn scarlet on
             banks gripped in
          that sweetest of all pain
makes the heart weep —
                    O once more
we've turned the winter
                  a new life can
spring from the sharpness of
            the green come back
             in the deep sleughs of man.

## The Northlands, Yellowknife: N.W.T.
## The Canadian Shield


There's nothing but rock here
bare, frost-shattered, bleak
and nine months under frost at that
hardness in hardness wrapped
                              men speak
of the cruel
                    the savage
                              land
long bye-passed
                    ignored
                              an emptiness
not only in map
                              but mind
              yet
heartland to heart if we
                              could only be
              as enduring
              sure
as this plateau of long grief
              that's still
    (though honed with wind
grooved plucked with eroding time)
guardian of past fire.
                              With hot magma in
                                each vein —

what gold we Oh! might
              out of ourselves
                              mine.

### The Northlands, Old Crow: Y.T.

Old Crow
         pickled in cold
              at fifty below
shingled with frost
              shuttered with snow
explodes in a springtime shout of boys
such as only a long winter's end
              ever, but ever, knows:
snow's the Canadian wonder —
           to
match this, and last it out
is to know
a shout of beauty that
carries the ice out and
breaks bud across the land.
Dogs bark
         women sing
birds are back in the air
only the fierce cold could
         make such a joy appear.

**One people, one country, one. . . .**

Born
     not of rock
              (the structure of fault and fold)
nor even of
        blood
              (the temper that men inherit)
                but
of *will*
     the will to be
             and to be one
this, Canada, is our root, and the flower of it, too.
We grew against the grain —
          not at one
          but at odds
             with
our geography:   that was the first pang.
                Our birth
had to breech mountains
            had the pain in it
of wildness parted
            the forest cut through
before the way was plain.
What was worse
        the darkness of
            long winter
              the bleak cold
                had, *had*
to be endured — ice in the channels of
our afflicted thoughts had to be thawed out.
Look at us.
        Our first was
        in islands, in presque îles, hacked off
from the main body of the country by
            mountains with spruce-sharp hackles up
and the storming or ice-shod Atlantic bights:
        here we
        it's true
built beside shattered firths

                         our bush-besieged garrisons
Old World divisions entrenching New World divides
citadel to outflank citadel, Louisburg/Halifax
Beausejour/Lawrence, with Micmac and Malecite
caught into the fray —
                         the array of all our arrogance,
yet
      drew from the silver seas nets of undreamed wealth,
not least the wealth of courage, hope
of what in fact found in us the common faith
to turn the vacant gulfs into the full-keeled routes
of the voyaging mind.
                         Drawn by the same love
the same longing for freedom to
                         make of the same wide emptiness
our at last fulfilment, see
how like we were,
                   though at swords drawn,
                                            in
our common adventuring:
                         havens to be made harbours
                         trails to be cut
                              the cross upraised
Malecite and Micmac drawn into charted ways
                   the quayside made alive
with the commerce of new joy — we were
makers of a new earth, struck like a medal with
the image of a
              looked-forward-to
                              new reign.
Dwell on this:   the basic unity
of two great people warring not so much
                         under the old and jealous flags
                                       as
beneath the banner of this cultivating task
carrying Jerusalem
                   bearing Athens
                              planting Rome
among the waste spaces crying out for use,

alike unlocking the power in unspent streams
in unlearned soil alike seeding the bread of life
from unthought woods working alike
house, barn, fence, mill, tool, machine
alike unleashing the pent-up drive of fuels,
                    alike
metalled with the force of unexploited ore.
Here were like paths
                    which,

                              crossing and again,
helped each and the other to push through
                              undiscovered passes to
the common heartland —
                              i.e., the waiting Canadas.
Locked in the unfruitful struggle of
                    Huron and Iroquois
waters went cargo-less that called for trade
rapids turned no mills
                              towns lay unborn in uncut pine
                              iron in the rock was still,
but hammered by French/British skill
                    grew into hulls
                    that laced the land
with the traffic of like questing:
                              speak of this.


Not the contentions of tongue, church, school, philosophy
                    but
the essential onenesses —
                              the philosophy of
                              man against the wilderness
                              the self against the world
which O made marvels of the land
                              the thrust-in saw
                              the biting drill
                              above all, the running routes
what (in Quebec, Ontario both)
                    in making the land over
                              made over men.
Launched on the Great River, this

                        was alike our school
            learning the white water
                        the long soo
                together:
                together
driving diversions through impeding rock
                        to make way for
                        the nosing ships pushed Europe in
to the American gut
giving the lakes a meaning
                        and streams, an end
turning the vain thunder of Niagara
(which Indians but stood to stare and wonder at)
                        with the stepped power
of lock on lock climbing the cut-back scarp,
to make an empire of engineered increase.
This was the faith that raised
                        steeples enough to top
                        maple, oak, pine
and ring out over marsh and forest with
                        bells of beatitude
bringing not alone Bethlehem but
                        Le Havre, Liverpool
the grace and prowess of our shared world to
the shores of Mattawa, French River, Georgian Bay
Mackinac, the English River, and at length the Red,
link by link tying stream and lake into
the network of the visionary hope.
And at the Red
                (the keystone of
                        our together arching will
to tie in coast to coast)
                        the West became
the language of our longing: to make the unploughed sod
                a spill of wealth such as
                        Assiniboine, Sioux
had never dreamed of,
                turning the black soil, gold.
Here men spoke
anticipation only
                acclamation
                        pride

76

pushing from Montreal — northwest,
                          from Hudson Bay, south
matching the long-crossed lines of
                          French, English penetration to
open out shut-in places
                          to the lingua franca of world-wide trade,
                          till
even the Chipewyan, the Blackfeet were
(malgré frost hail or drought that kept them back)
caught in the changed climate of far ends.
And, last, at the Pacific rim
                          though probed by British sail
                                    deep into the mountains with
                                              the running and silver tides
Musqueam and Squamish knew,
what burst from beyond the mountains
                          by that mad course
                          piercing Hell's gate itself
took the joint spirit of
Scotch factor and French coureurs des bois
                          to at length make —
                                    plunging to history and
                                              a new geography,
unknown to coast-bound Nootka, or
                          gripped-by-mountain Kootenai.
Here with the speech and faith
                          of common courage
                          of together strength
                          of the one and at-one-making dream
a mari usque ad mare
they rounded the great adventure out.
Inseparable in what they did to draw
                          the separate together
(the bits and pieces of the fragmented land
                          by seas divided
                          by mountains split)
shall French and British, who made the marvel of
                          one country here,

now from the apartness of their ancient hates
                    let it all
                    O fall
                    O fall
                    apart?
Summons the binding forces up
            flung railways across divides
            linked straits to land-locked plains
                made this land one
to do no less over thd divides of *man:*
*will* the thinking
            (splintered by tongues)
                                again one
the longing
            (by creeds split)
                                one again
one people, one country, one hope, one wonder, one. . . . .